Take a Look!
Modern Media Literacy

# Creating Content



Julie Knutson

CHERRY LAKE PRESS

Published in the United States of America by Cherry Lake Publishing Group
Ann Arbor, Michigan
www.cherrylakepublishing.com

Reading Adviser: Beth Walker Gambro, MS, Ed., Reading Consultant, Yorkville, IL
Content Adviser: Kristin Fontichiaro, Clinical Professor, University of Michigan School of Information

Photo Credits: © Xavier Lorenzo/Shutterstock, cover, title page; © Wayhome Studio/Shutterstock, 5; © AnnJane/Shutterstock, 6; © Shyamalamuralinath/Shutterstock, 7; © New Africa/Shutterstock, 8; © Fabio Principe/Shutterstock, 9; © Prostock-studio/Shutterstock, 10; © Joyseulay/Shutterstock, 11; © Iryna Imago/Shutterstock, 12; © Poetra.RH/Shutterstock, 13; © Xavier Lorenzo/Shutterstock, 15, 17, 18; © Xavier Lorenzo/Shutterstock, 22, 23; © LightField Studios/Shutterstock, 25; © Elnur/Shutterstock, 26; © fast-stock/Shutterstock, 28; © SeventyFour/Shutterstock, 29; © Nomad_Soul/Shutterstock, 31



**Cherry Lake Press** is an imprint of Cherry Lake Publishing Group.

Library of Congress Cataloging-in-Publication Data

Names: Knutson, Julie, author.
Title: Creating content / written by Julie Knutson.
Description: Ann Arbor, Michigan : Cherry Lake Publishing, [2025] | Series: Take a look! Modern media literacy | Audience: Grades 4-6 | Summary: "Creating Content takes readers through the process of creating and sharing content in a responsible, inclusive way."—Provided by publisher.
Identifiers: LCCN 2024035956 | ISBN 9781668956304 (hardcover) | ISBN 9781668957158 (paperback) | ISBN 9781668958025 (ebook) | ISBN 9781668958896 (pdf)
Subjects: LCSH: Media literacy—Juvenile literature. | Content analysis (Communication)—Juvenile literature. | Mass media—Audiences—Juvenile literature.
Classification: LCC P96.M4 K583 2025 | DDC 302.23—dc23/eng/20240905
LC record available at https://lccn.loc.gov/2024035956

Cherry Lake Press would like to acknowledge the work of the Partnership for 21st Century Learning, a Network of Battelle for Kids. Please visit Battelle for Kids online for more information.

Printed in the United States of America

Note from publisher: Websites change regularly, and their future contents are outside of our control. Supervise children when conducting any recommended online searches for extended learning opportunities.

**Julie Knutson** (she/her) is an author and educator who lives and works in Philadelphia, PA. She's no stranger to navigating media in our modern world, and she teaches her students to do the same. Whether working with students to craft interview questions or debating designs for a classroom magazine, she also loves guiding middle schoolers through the media-making process.

# CONTENTS

CHAPTER 1

# Take a Look! The Big Picture

262,800,000 hours. That's the amount of content uploaded to YouTube each year. Break this down? That's 500-plus hours of video uploaded *every minute*!

Today, humans produce more content—video and otherwise—than at any other point in history. In the past, only a small number of people could publish music, videos, and books. You needed special skills and expensive resources to create **media**. That's not how it is anymore! With technology, it's easier than ever to share your thoughts with people far and wide.

Many podcasters release audio *and* video podcasts. Technology has made it possible to make and share both easily!

Millions of memes are made and shared online.
They share ideas, reactions, and jokes.

## What Counts as Content?

Just what do we mean when we talk about *content*? Content is publicly shared creative material. Podcasts. Articles. Memes. These are all forms of content.

Whether official or unofficial, people make content for a variety of purposes. It might be to inform others about a topic. It could be to persuade people. Or it could simply be to entertain. Sometimes it's a combination of all three.

Not all media is digital. Printed books, newspapers, and magazines are also media.

Print ads in magazines are considered legacy media content.

Newspaper articles can be in print or online.

People make content to communicate. People **consume** content for information or entertainment. The two main categories are legacy media content and social media content, which is also called user-generated content. Legacy media content includes content from media sources like radio broadcasting, print ads, books, movies, and TV.

Creating legacy content often requires many people working together. Think about a newsroom. There, staffers take set steps to research, write, and review this type of content. They typically follow a process to make sure that what gets shared is accurate.

Anyone can post on social media as long as they follow social media platform rules.

Many legacy media creators also have social media channels. However, social media content can be made by anyone. It can range from YouTube videos to Instagram reels. Some people who post on social media work for a sponsor or a company. Their content must be approved by their employers. Other people who post content on social media don't need to get clearance before they share.

In most cases, there's no expert checking information before people post on social media. If people believe what an influencer is saying, they see the influencer as an authority. Gossip and false information can easily spread. Just because something goes viral doesn't mean it's real. It doesn't mean it's true. You may see tons of views on a video and think it *must* have important information. But be careful what sources you trust! The video creator may—or may not—know what they're sharing is incorrect.

Read on to learn more about how and why content gets made and about the rights and responsibilities that content creators have.

## GROW & ENGAGE

**Everyone can use social media. How could you inspire others to engage with information on social media in a safe way? How could you inspire them to be responsible with what they share on social media?**

Are there ways that a creator could use AI responsibly when creating? How might these creators use AI responsibly?

# USING AI TO CREATE

**Morals** are rules that a culture agrees on. These rules are about what's right and wrong. **Ethics** is the study of these. Something is ethical if it follows a culture's morals. Is using **generative artificial intelligence** (GenAI) to create content ethical? There are many different opinions.

Some people think of GenAI as a tool. They say a tool can't be unethical. But they think using it to harm others would make it unethical. Other people think that using GenAI in general is unethical. People claim companies trained GenAI with other people's work. They didn't have permission to use these materials. Usually, using other people's work without permission is illegal. If AI doesn't respect people's ownership of their own work, is using it ethical?

Some people think using GenAI could be good for creators. *Forbes* is an American business magazine. Bernard Marr, a *Forbes* columnist, writes a lot about AI. He says GenAI could help creators. GenAI generates content based on a prompt. Marr believes it creates "new" material when it does this. Others disagree. Marr encourages the ethical use of all AI.

So what do you think? Is the use of GenAI to create content ethical?

CHAPTER 2

# Break It Down! What Content Creators Consider

Meet Max! This student content creator recently launched a YouTube channel. His purpose? To create fun videos on content relevant to him and his friends.

Max has been learning about how to create great content online. He wants to make a top 10 ranking video for chip flavors.

To prepare, Max wants to watch other top 10 videos about food to see what other creators have done. He searches for food videos with more than 10,000 views. These creators have ranked everything from snacks to desserts.

Max's friends use YouTube all the time. They love sharing funny videos with each other.

He feels like he has a good idea of what a successful top 10 food video looks like. He now knows he wants to give good reasons for his choices. He also wants to make people laugh.

Here are five excellent questions every creator should ask as they plan:

1. **What am I creating?** This question concerns both content and **format**. What will you create? How will you present it? Why are you making it?

2. **For whom am I creating it?** Who is your audience? How will you capture their interest? How will you keep it? What different **rhetorical appeals** will you use?

3. **Does my message work with the format and technology used?** How will the message be visually presented? What technology and tools do you need?

4. **Which values, lifestyles, and points of view are represented in my content? Which are not?** What's your **viewpoint**? What values are you expressing?

5. **Have I communicated my purpose effectively?** This is a question for reviewing your rough draft. Is your core message clear? Are you ready to share your content?

Doing creative research can be fun. It's good to have examples of the media you want to make in your mind when you start creating.

After Max plans his video, he does a few practice runs before he hits record.

Max thinks through these steps for his video:

1. **What am I creating?** Max is set on his top 10 ranking video for chip flavors. He also went into this knowing his format—a YouTube video. He knows his friends don't spend very much time on TikTok or Instagram. But they do watch a LOT of YouTube videos. Max wants to entertain people! He wants to make his friends laugh.

2. **For whom am I creating it?** Max's audience is other people his age. He thinks he knows what they'll like. He knows he can talk in a casual way. He also knows how most kids his age already feel about this topic. Some love classic chip flavors. Some love the flaming hot flavors that make their eyes water. He's ready to make them all laugh.

## SHARE & ENGAGE

The phrase "digital footprint" refers to the information about you that you leave behind from your activity online. Why is a positive digital footprint important? How can you build a positive digital footprint when sharing new media you create? When viewing the media other people create?

3. **Is my message enhanced by the format and technology used?** Yes! Max thinks a YouTube video will best get his message across. He wants to use some facts to support his choices. He also thinks he'll use some sad, disgusted faces when talking about the worst flavors (here's looking at you, salt and vinegar!).

4. **Which values, lifestyles, and points of view are represented in my content? Which are not?** Max knows that his point of view on chips will be in the video. He knows his snack-loving lifestyle will be shown in the video too. Max values humor. He also values a tasty chip! These values will show in the video.

5. **Have I communicated my purpose effectively?** Max makes the first draft of his video. He reviews it. He wrote a script ahead of time to help him practice. He chose words and a **tone** that will make his peers laugh. He explained his reasons for his chip rankings. He thinks he communicated his purpose effectively.

# CAN CREATORS POST ANYTHING THEY WANT?

In the United States, everyone is guaranteed freedom of speech. But that's not the freedom to say whatever you want wherever you want. Speech that harms others is not allowed. You can't threaten or **harass** other people. You can't disrupt school or government operations.

Social media companies have the right and responsibility to set up rules for how users engage on their platforms.

YouTube has community guidelines and policies. These guidelines and policies cover everything from medical **misinformation** to inappropriate language. Content promoting things like hate speech, graphic violence, and dangerous behavior aren't allowed. TikTok has community guidelines. Instagram has community guidelines, too.

So creators can't post anything they want to on social media. They need to be aware of the rules and laws in place. Remember, these can change over time. Make sure you know about these rules and laws before you choose to create or post content. Be responsible with what you create!

Max has a lot of fun recording his video. Making content you're proud of takes time! Max has put a lot of time into this project.

## CREATE & INQUIRE

With an adult, go online to gather all of the information you can on a current event issue. Then search the issue on social media. View one of the first pieces of media that pops up. Did the creator miss certain facts? Did they not include an important perspective? Come up with a plan to create your own media that will fill in the knowledge gaps you find.

Part of the process of creating content also happens *after* the first draft. Max now has to edit his video. He chooses to add music in the background. He adds some animations. He adds some sound effects.

Next? He needs to upload the video to YouTube. He can choose for his video to be private or public. Once that's done, he can finally share his video!

CHAPTER 3

# Show What You Know! Create Your Own Content

As citizens of the 21st century, you're swimming in a sea of content! You consume it *and* you create it. You get to choose how to do both of those things responsibly.

You interact with media every day. If you have a phone or a tablet, you probably use YouTube. You may have other social media accounts like TikTok, Instagram, Snapchat, or Twitch. You may read books or watch the news. Maybe you just view and read media other people have created. That's okay! It's important to know what goes into creating content to understand the media you consume. If you don't like the way the media was made, maybe you'll choose not to watch or read it.

Most people use both online and offline media. You can make both, too. Set your media-making goals and get going!

A good place to start when creating content? Brainstorming. You can try writing down all of your ideas and sorting through them when you're done.

## THINK & EXPLORE

**Good content is always created with an audience in mind. Find a magazine that's written for young readers, like *The Week Junior* or *TIME for Kids*. Then find a magazine aimed at adults, such as *TIME* or *Newsweek*. What similarities do you notice in their design—fonts, colors, images, graphics? What differences do you see? How do you think these magazines considered their audiences when creating their content?**

Maybe you create your own media. In that case, it's helpful to know what you're doing. Are you interested in blogging? Making videos? Writing news articles or recording podcasts? No matter the kind of media, use your knowledge about how to create to make something great.

You can use the steps Max used in Chapter 2 to create your own media. Ask questions about the content and format of what you're creating. Think through why you're making it in the first place. Consider your audience and how you can appeal to them. Think about how format can enhance your message. Think about what values, viewpoints, and **bias** are present in your media. And once you have a rough draft, ask if you communicated what you wanted to.

What's a current event issue you care about? Research it online. Note the different content formats you see.

It's important to ask questions about the content you create and the content you see and hear. Want to navigate this sea of content without sinking? Just use what you've learned! You're the one steering the ship.

# YOUTH MEDIA!

Through PBS NewsHour's Student Reporting Labs (SRL), kids and teens create content on everything from book bans to baseball.

Each year, the SRL team shares a list of critical topics. In response to these prompts, student **journalists** create media. Their products range from **profiles** and explainer videos to podcasts. Recent topics include "Statues, Symbols, and Stories," which asks kids to think about how we remember the past.

Want to learn more about this hands-on program? Visit PBS's Student Reporting Lab website with an adult. Share the site with your teachers and friends. Discuss how you can build a strong group of ethical media makers!

# Do More!

## Extension Activity

Maybe you want to record a podcast about video game mods. Perhaps you want to make a video to teach people how to design pollinator-friendly gardens. Regardless of the topic, you can learn a lot from the people around you. Interviews can be a great first step to gathering content!

- **Research the person.** Who are you talking to? What is their area of expertise? How do they know what they know?
- **Write questions.** Don't write questions that can be answered with *yes* or *no*. Use *who, what, when, where, why,* and *how* as starters. You can also start questions with words like *describe* and *explain*.
- **Gather your materials and set a time and place.** What will you need to record your interview? Where and when will it take place? Share all these details with your interviewee.
- **Record your interview.** You'll need to record audio of the interview if you're going to make it into a podcast. And of course, you'll need to record a video if that's your end goal. Make sure you get permission from the interviewee before you press record!
- **Edit your interview.** Piece together your audio or video. Edit out long silences. Maybe add some music. Create an introduction. Add commentary. Add a conclusion.

What to do next? Share what you've made! When you've created responsible media that you're proud of, the natural next step is to share it.

# Learn More

## On the Web

Search these online sources with an adult:

- Common Sense Media—Connecting with Purpose: Digital Footprint | Digital Connections
- Teen Voices: Oversharing and Your Digital Footprint | Common Sense Education | Video
- What is Digital Citizenship? | CBC Kids | Video

## Glossary

**bias** (BIE-uhs) prejudice in favor of or against a thing, person, or group

**consume** (kuhn-SOOM) to engage with; to use

**ethics** (EH-thiks) the philosophical study of morals

**format** (FOR-mat) the way that something is arranged

**generative artificial intelligence** (JEH-nuh-ruh-tive ar-tuh-FIH-shuhl in-TEH-luh-juhns) computer programs that input data from sources on the internet and then output different combinations of that data

**harass** (huh-RAAS) to scare or pressure someone

**journalists** (JUHR-nuh-lists) people who write or report media stories

**media** (MEE-dee-uh) means of communicating information to large numbers of people, including television, newspapers, magazines, and radio

**misinformation** (mis-in-fuhr-MAY-shuhn) false information spread by people who don't realize it is false and who share it without meaning to cause harm

**morals** (MOHR-uhlz) culturally agreed upon rules about what's right and wrong

**profiles** (PROH-fiylz) articles about people

**rhetorical appeals** (rih-TOR-ih-kuhl uh-PEELZ) qualities of an argument that persuade people to support it

**tone** (TOHN) style of writing or speaking used to achieve a result or communicate an emotion

**values** (VAL-yooz) ideas or beliefs that are important to a person and that guide their life

**viewpoint** (VYOO-poynt) way of seeing the world

## Index